Welcome to So Yummy's Cook Smarter, Not Harder: Ingenious Recipe Hacks! We've assembled our absolute best expert tips and game-changing tricks in one place, so you can live your best life in the kitchen.

These hacks are guaranteed to save you time, alleviate stress, and make cooking delicious food fun. You'll find simple step-by-step instructions for mouthwatering appetizers, snacks, and meals, as well as insanely yummy desserts of all kinds, from cookies and brownies to ice cream and cakes.

There's nothing same-old about any of these recipes. Each dish incorporates at least one hack that'll become part of your kitchen repertoire forever— a twist your guests will remember and want to replicate.

Like to bake? We've got biscuit hacks, pie hacks, and cookie hacks galore. Love a gadget? We've got muffin tin hacks, mason jar hacks, and ice-tray hacks. Entertaining? We've got breakfast and brunch hacks, cocktail and dessert hacks. Need we go on? We could, but instead, flip through these pages and you'll discover a gazillion ways to up your kitchen game.

Even better: This book is totally interactive. In addition to some of our most popular recipes that over 40 million fans are loving online (you can scan dishes to access them on your mobile device), we've also packed in extra wow factor: Exclusive Content icons on brand-new recipes and QR codes for our first ever how-to videos hosted by So Yummy experts. You won't find these anywhere else!

For more recipes and videos visit So Yummy on Facebook, Instagram, and at SoYummy.com.

So Yummy!

COOK SMARTER, NOT HARDER

Ingenious Recipe Hacks

Dedicated to our fans who love creative cooking hacks and having fun in the kitchen

So Yummy!

COOK SMARTER, NOT HARDER

Ingenious Recipe Hacks

TABLE OF CONTENTS

06
Kitchen Essentials

08
5-Ingredient Pull-Apart Sausage Rolls

12
Stuffed Avocado Egg Cups

16
Lazy Girl Mason Jar Omelette

20
Baked Bruschetta Boats

24
Sweet and Savory Pancake Muffins

SAUSAGE ROLLS PG. 8

28
#NotSorry Fried Breakfast Sausage Egg

32
One-Pan Egg in a Biscuit

36
Hostess with the Mostest Omelette Rolls

40
Bacon, Egg, and Cheese Brunch Dip

44
Pizza-For-Breakfast Quiche

48
Summer-Lovin' Cherry Pie Bites

ROSÉ LEMONADE PG. 15

Easy step-by-step recipes for seriously delicious meals, plus cooking hacks you need in your life.

52 Mochi Ice Cream

56 Molten Lava Cubes

60 All-The-Edges Brownies

MASON JAR OMELETTE PG. 16

64 Double-Dip Brownie Ice Cream Pops

68 Fudgy Pretzel Crust Brownies

72 #TBT Cookies and Cream Crunch Bombs

76 Crispy Cheesecake Bites

80 Strawberry Ice Cream Crispwiches

84 Smart Cookie Hacks

90 Coco-Orange Ice Pops

94 Furry Cookie Monster Cake

98 Fresh Flower Cascade Cake

102 Straight Fire Cake

EDGES BROWNIES PG. 60

WHAT TO LOOK FOR ON OUR PAGES

FUN FACT
Origin stories and other juicy info about your favorite dishes and ingredients.

MAKE IT VEGGIE
Modify a recipe for the vegetarians in your life.

MAKE IT VEGAN
Suggestions for vegan-friendly swaps!

EXCLUSIVE CONTENT
Brand-new expert tutorials and So Yummy recipes you won't find anywhere else!

Watch the recipe video

60

SERVES 6-10

5-INGREDIENT PULL-APART SAUSAGE ROLLS

This **extra-indulgent** brunch dish is also extra-easy to make.

INGREDIENTS:

2 sheets puff pastry

1 wheel Camembert

30 cooked pork sausage balls

Sesame seeds

1 egg, lightly beaten

"

I'm vegetarian, so when making this dish for myself, I use veggie meatballs in place of the sausage. You can also use veggie breakfast links—cut them in half and use a couple pieces for each section—but keep in mind you won't get that perfectly round look.

—Tennille

STEP 1

STEP 2

STEP 3

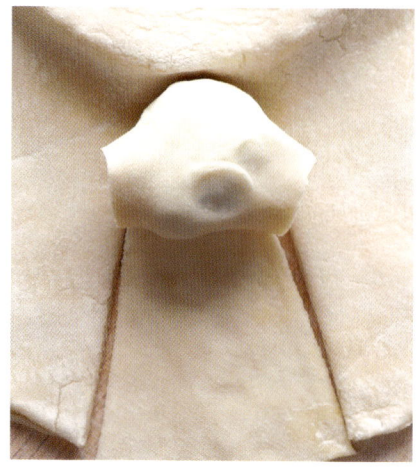

STEP 4

STEP 5

STEP 6

DIRECTIONS:

1. Preheat the oven to **350°**. Lay out one sheet of pastry and place the cheese wheel in the center.

2. Cover with the second sheet of pastry, and evenly place the sausage balls around the pastry edge. Make pastry cuts between each sausage.

3. Wrap the top layer of pastry around the sausage and roll to the center.

4. Repeat for all sausages, then add more balls around the bottom layer of pastry. Wrap and roll toward the center.

5. Brush on the egg wash, top with sesame seeds, and bake for **40 minutes**.

6. Remove from the oven and gently remove the top layer of the center pastry to reveal the gooey cheese dip. Serve warm.

Use all store-bought ingredients and you can pull this off in 10 minutes (plus baking time).

PAIR IT WITH
TIPSY ARNOLD PALMER

This boozy version of the summer refresher can be enjoyed year-round.

INGREDIENTS:

3 oz chilled lemonade
3 oz iced tea
1.5 oz vodka
Fresh peach slices, for garnish
Mint sprigs, for garnish

If peaches aren't in season, add lemon slices and lemonade ice cubes.

DIRECTIONS:

1. In a glass over ice, add the lemonade, iced tea, and vodka. Stir to combine.
2. Garnish with peaches and mint, and serve.

Watch the recipe video

SERVES 2

STUFFED AVOCADO EGG CUPS

Avo-cadabra! These unexpected **breakfast bowls** are chock-full of healthy fats.

INGREDIENTS:

2 avocados

4 eggs

Salt and pepper

TOPPINGS:

Crushed red pepper

Bacon

Shredded cheddar and chopped chives

Chopped bell pepper and basil

"

You can bake these as little or as long as you want, depending on how runny or done you like your eggs. Anywhere from 7 to 15 minutes—you want to make sure your cheese melts.

— Tennille

STEP 1

STEP 2

STEP 3

STEP 4

STEP 5

DIRECTIONS:

1. Preheat the oven to **375°**. Halve the avocados and remove the pits. Using the flip side of a muffin tin, place the avocado halves between the cups.

2. Scoop out a bit more of the avocado to make more room for fillings.

3. Break an egg into the center of each avocado. Add salt and pepper.

4. Season with your choice of toppings.

5. Bake for about **15 minutes**, let cool slightly, and serve.

EXCLUSIVE CONTENT!

PAIR IT WITH
ROSÉ LEMONADE

Frozen watermelon ups the ante on your pretty pink brunch drink.

Pour it in the blender and whip up a frosé!

INGREDIENTS:

Frozen watermelon cubes
3 oz chilled rosé
3 oz chilled lemonade
Splash of seltzer
Lemon slice, for garnish

DIRECTIONS:

1. Place watermelon cubes in your glass.
2. Pour in the rosé and lemonade, and top with seltzer splash and lemon.

MAKE IT VEGGIE

Leave out the ham! If you'd like some added protein and flavor, chop up a link of your favorite meatless sausage.

Watch the recipe video

SERVES 1

LAZY GIRL MASON JAR OMELETTE

Shaken not stirred—if you haven't mastered the art of making **eggs in the microwave**, you haven't been living your life right.

INGREDIENTS:

3 eggs

TOPPINGS:

Chopped spinach

Sliced grape tomatoes

Diced bell pepper

Chopped ham

Shredded cheddar

Salt and pepper

If you have time, sauté your chopped spinach before you assemble the jar. It'll make for a tastier omelette.

– Katie

STEP 1

STEP 2

STEP 3

STEP 4

DIRECTIONS:

1. Break the eggs into your empty mason jar.
2. Add your toppings of choice plus the salt and pepper to taste.
3. Screw on the top and shake to blend the egg and combine.
4. When you're ready to eat, remove the top and put the open jar in the microwave for **2 minutes** (don't put metal in the microwave!). Let cool slightly, fluff with your fork, and dig in.

Your mason jar is a super-savvy kitchen tool, use it to cook eggs, make ice cream (page 67), or cut dough (page 20)!

HOW TO
KEEP YOUR GREENS FRESHER LONGER

No time for slime! Scan here to watch our hack for extending the life of your lettuce.

Watch the recipe video

SERVES 4

BAKED BRUSCHETTA BOATS

You don't even need knife skills to pull off this **impressive**, **crowd-pleasing** pastry appetizer.

INGREDIENTS:

2 sheets puff pastry

10 Roma tomatoes, chopped

1 small onion, chopped

1 small bunch basil, chopped

4 slices fresh mozzarella

"

This is such an easy app to put together—the mason jar lid gives you perfect circles in seconds. Be sure to pinch the sides of the dough boats tightly so they don't open up while baking.

— Tennille

STEP 1

STEP 2

STEP 3

STEP 4

STEP 5

DIRECTIONS:

1. Preheat the oven to **350°**. Lay out one sheet of pastry. Using a wide-mouth mason jar lid, cut out circles.

2. Roll the edges of each circle toward the center and pinch the ends together creating a boat. Repeat with the second sheet.

3. Combine your tomatoes, onion, and basil to make the bruschetta. Spoon the mixture into each boat. Place the boats in concentric circles inside a parchment-lined round cake pan, leaving the center open.

4. Place the mozzarella slices in the center and bake for **25 minutes**.

5. Remove from the pan and place on a platter. Serve warm so the cheese will be gooey for dipping.

MAKE-YOUR-OWN
BRUNCH BRUSCHETTA BAR

First, slice and toast your bread, and brush it with olive oil.
Then arrange these ingredients on your table or platter
(be sure to include serving utensils) and let your guests do their thing.

SPREAD

| Ricotta Cheese |  Crushed Avocado |  Nut Butter |  Basil Pesto |

TOPPING

| Cured Meats |  Soft-Boiled Eggs |  Raspberries |  Arugula |

GARNISH

| Diced Tomatoes |  Red Onions |  Mint |  Chopped Walnuts |

Also on the table

Salt and Pepper — Olive Oil and Vinegar — Chili Flakes — Honey

Watch the recipe video

SERVES 6-8

SWEET & SAVORY PANCAKE MUFFINS

Basically an entire **breakfast in muffin** form—these will satisfy every craving and they're great on the go.

INGREDIENTS:

8 breakfast sausage links, uncooked, sliced in half crosswise

12 Medjool dates, pitted

2 cups pancake mix, prepared

"

You can replace the sausage with your favorite breakfast meat, or if you're vegetarian, leave it out altogether and just include the dates. Don't forget a side of syrup for dipping!

— Logan

STEP 1

STEP 2

STEP 3

STEP 4

DIRECTIONS:

1. Preheat the oven to **350°**. Place 2 sausage pieces in each cup of a nonstick 12-cup muffin tin. Bake for about **15 minutes**, until browned.

2. Remove the tin from the oven, and place a date on top of the sausage in each cup.

3. Pour the pancake batter into each cup to fill.

4. Bake for **25 minutes**, let cool slightly, and serve.

EXCLUSIVE CONTENT!

More, more, more!

Pancake muffins are super versatile—you can switch them up with seasonal fruit, or make them vegetarian-friendly. Scan here for lots more ideas!

Watch the recipe video

SERVES 4

#NotSorry
FRIED BREAKFAST SAUSAGE EGG

Yes, you read that right. Also known as a **Scotch egg**, it's literally wrapped in sausage and deep-fried. Yum.

INGREDIENTS:

1 lb bulk pork breakfast sausage

2 eggs, lightly beaten, plus 4 soft-boiled eggs, cooled and peeled

1½ cups breadcrumbs

1 tsp salt

½ tsp pepper

Vegetable oil, for frying

> This is one of my favorite grab-and-go recipes because I'm always on the run. If you have time, elevate it a bit by mixing up some sriracha mayo as a dipping sauce.
>
> – Logan

STEP 1

STEP 2

STEP 3

STEP 4

DIRECTIONS:

1. Prep four small bowls for your assembly line: sausage, boiled eggs, beaten eggs, and breadcrumbs. Flatten about ¼ of the sausage into a patty. Wrap it around a boiled egg, patting gently, to cover completely.

2. Dip the egg into the beaten eggs, then the breadcrumbs to coat. Repeat with the other eggs.

3. Heat the oil to **350°**. Fry the eggs for about **5 minutes**, until sausage is cooked through and eggs are golden brown.

4. Drain on paper towel and serve.

FUN FACT

In not-so-humble beginnings, Scotch eggs were conceived as a pocket-size snack for well-off picnickers and travelers in the 1700s. London food hall Fortnum and Mason takes credit for coming up with them and packing them in the elaborate baskets it still sells today. But over time the diminutive dish has also garnered mass appeal, becoming a staple at the pub, at brunch, and yes, at picnics. And there's nothing Scottish about it—scotched is an old-school way of describing the minced meat surrounding the egg.

SERVES 4-8

ONE-PAN EGG IN A BISCUIT

Buttery, **flaky**, and **cheesy**: This recipe checks all our boxes for a perfect breakfast.

INGREDIENTS:

1 can refrigerated biscuit dough

¼ cup melted butter

½ cup shredded cheddar cheese

2 tbsp chopped fresh chives

4 eggs

2 tsp paprika, optional

"

We don't like to waste any part of a good biscuit! When cutting out the holes for your eggs, be sure to save the scraps—they're great for dunking into perfectly runny yolks.

— *Tess*

STEP 1

STEP 2

STEP 3

STEP 4

DIRECTIONS:

1. Preheat the oven according to the biscuit package instructions. Lay the biscuits on your baking pan. Brush melted butter onto each and sprinkle with cheese and chives.

2. Using a small biscuit cutter or circle cookie cutter, remove the center of each biscuit and place it on the pan. Into each hole, crack an egg.

3. Sprinkle paprika and bake according to the package instructions, until biscuits are golden and cheese is melted.

4. Let cool slightly and serve with biscuit tops for dipping!

{ *If you don't like a runny egg, go ahead and scramble it. You can even add a diced-up veggie for an omelette vibe.* }

ADD THIS TO YOUR BREAKFAST

Waffle-Iron Bacon

Origami your way to the most impressive breakfast side dish ever. Scan here to watch our hack.

MAKE IT VEGGIE

This recipe is super adaptable. You can leave out the meat and add some fresh herbs to amp up the flavor.

Watch the recipe video

SERVES 6-8

HOSTESS WITH THE MOSTEST OMELETTE ROLLS

Talk about **brunch goals**: Let us present mini omelettes sandwiched between garlic knots.

INGREDIENTS:

1 dozen frozen garlic knots, baked

10 eggs

1 cup cherry tomatoes, sliced

1 cup sliced mushrooms

1 cup diced peppers

1 cup cubed ham

2 cups grated cheddar

1 tsp salt

½ tsp pepper

"

We took a dessert approach to breakfast—a giant sheet pan of scrambled eggs and fillings, topped with cheese, rolled up like a Swiss roll cake. The trickiest part is rolling without cracking. Be sure to spray the pan well, don't overcook the eggs, and roll while the eggs are still warm so they're pliable.

– Rachel

STEP 1

STEP 2

STEP 3

STEP 4

STEP 5

DIRECTIONS:

1. Preheat the oven to **350°**. Grease a 9 x 13-inch baking pan. Break the eggs onto the sheet and whisk.

2. Add tomatoes, mushrooms, peppers, ham, cheese, salt, and pepper. Bake for **15 minutes**.

3. Let cool slightly, then roll into a tight spiral.

4. Slice the roll into 12 equal pieces.

5. Place one slice between a halved garlic knot. Repeat for all knots, and serve.

EXCLUSIVE CONTENT

Fluffy Omelettes 101

Making great eggs is a life skill worth perfecting.
Scan here and let us share our secrets.

Watch the recipe video

SERVES 2-4

BACON, EGG, AND CHEESE BRUNCH DIP

You use these **ingredients on the daily**, but we bet you've never combined them like this.

INGREDIENTS:

6 frozen garlic knots, thawed

8 oz softened cream cheese

1½ cups sour cream

1½ cups shredded cheddar cheese

½ cup cooked and chopped bacon

2 tbsp chopped chives

4 eggs, softly scrambled

> The hack is to use the bowl to hold your chips in place. When you remove it, your dip has a nice landing spot! Be sure to slice the knots thin so the chips will be crispy, not chewy.
>
> – Rachel

STEP 1

STEP 2

STEP 3

STEP 4

STEP 5

DIRECTIONS:

1. Preheat the oven to **350°**. Slice the knots thinly. Place the slices in a single layer on a 9 x 13-inch baking sheet. Bake for about **6 minutes**, until crisp.

2. In a medium bowl, combine the cream cheese, sour cream, 1 cup cheddar, bacon, and chives.

3. Fold in the scrambled eggs.

4. Place a small or medium bowl upside down in the center of an oven-safe pan. Arrange the bread slices around the bowl. Remove the bowl, fill the center with the egg mixture, and top with the remaining ½ cup cheddar.

5. Bake for **20 minutes**, until heated through and cheese is melted and bubbly. Serve warm.

EXCLUSIVE CONTENT!

PAIR IT WITH
SRIRACHA BLOODY MARY

It's all about that tangy, garlicky special sauce.

INGREDIENTS:

2 oz vodka
4 oz vegetable juice, like V8
1 tbsp fresh lemon juice
Horseradish, to taste
Worcestershire sauce, to taste
Sriracha, to taste
Pinch celery seed
Salt and pepper
Cornichons, pickled onions, and celery, for garnish

DIRECTIONS:

1. Add all ingredients to a shaker or glass and mix well.
2. Pour over ice and add garnish.

Freeze the cocktail in ice-pop molds for a boozy summer treat (see page 93).

MAKE IT VEGGIE

This could not be easier. Just choose a veggie pizza!

Watch the recipe video

SERVES 4-6

PIZZA-FOR-BREAKFAST QUICHE

How have you lived so long without combining **pizza** and **quiche**? We're here to fix that.

INGREDIENTS:

Frozen pizza of your choice, thawed

10 eggs

½ cup heavy cream

½ tsp salt

¼ tsp pepper

FUN FACT

Quiche was brunch before brunch was cool (or at least before it was Instafamous). The savory pie originated in northeastern France, hit peak popularity in America in the '70s and '80s, and remains a classic. The base of eggs and cream can be combined with any number of fillings (from bacon for a traditional quiche Lorraine to, yes, pizza toppings), poured into a crust, and baked. It's that easy. The dish is super versatile, and it's great for picnics and potlucks because it can be served at any temperature.

STEP 1

STEP 2

STEP 3

STEP 4

STEP 5

DIRECTIONS:

1. Preheat the oven to **350°**. Scrape all the toppings off your pizza and reserve them for later.

2. Press the crust into a nonstick pie pan.

3. In a large bowl or measuring cup, combine the eggs, cream, salt, pepper, and reserved pizza toppings until well mixed.

4. Pour the mixture into the pizza crust.

5. Bake for **40 minutes**, until the eggs have set and the crust is golden. If the crust browns too quickly, cover it loosely with aluminum foil. Let cool slightly and serve warm or at room temp.

PAIR IT WITH
ITALIAN ORANGE SODA

Sunshine in a glass.

INGREDIENTS:

2 cups fresh-squeezed orange juice
¾ cup sugar
Zest of 2 oranges (in big strips)
Seltzer, chilled

DIRECTIONS:

1. Simmer the OJ, sugar, and zest for about 20 minutes. Let cool and strain.

2. When ready to serve, add syrup to your glass with ice, pour in seltzer, and stir.

An ice-cube tray acts as your pie mold.

 Watch the recipe video

SERVES 6

SUMMER-LOVIN' CHERRY PIE BITES

Low-maintenance baking is about all we can manage on hot days—fill these sweet little snacks with seasonal fruit.

INGREDIENTS:

2 sheets store-bought pie dough, thawed

3 cups diced pitted cherries

1 cup sugar

2 eggs, lightly beaten

¼ cup sanding sugar

"

An ice tray is probably the most versatile tool you can have in your kitchen—see our Molten Lava Cubes (page 56) and Mochi Ice Cream (page 52). One of my favorite hacks is to pour in leftover coffee and freeze it. I pop the cubes into my iced coffee to keep it cold without watering it down.

— Logan

STEP 1

STEP 2

STEP 3

STEP 4

STEP 5

STEP 6

DIRECTIONS:

1. Preheat the oven to **375°**. In a medium bowl, combine the cherries and 1 cup sugar.

2. Use a dough sheet to cover your ice tray, and gently knuckle it into each pocket.

3. Scoop 1 tbsp cherry filling into each pocket. Brush egg wash onto the dough.

4. Add the second sheet of dough on top, and pinch to seal.

5. Flip the ice tray to release the pie nuggets. Separate them using a pizza cutter. Brush on the egg wash and sprinkle with sanding sugar.

6. Bake for **15 minutes**, let cool slightly, and serve.

In the fall, fill them with apples or spiced pumpkin.

HOW TO
PIT CHERRIES WITH A CHOPSTICK

No fancy gadgets necessary.

WHAT YOU NEED:

Cherries
Glass soda bottle
Chopstick

DIRECTIONS:

1. Set a cherry on top of the open soda bottle.
2. Use one hand to hold the bottle securely.
3. Use the other hand to hold the chopstick and punch the center of the cherry. The pit will drop right into the bottle!

+ plus freezing time
15
SERVES 6-12

MOCHI ICE CREAM

These **rice cake treats** are just plain adorable, and they're really fun to make and share—let the ice tray be your guide.

INGREDIENTS:

Cooking spray

2 cups rice flour

1 cup sugar

Strawberry, matcha, and mango ice cream, softened

Freeze-dried strawberries, matcha powder, and freeze-dried mango, for garnish

"

Glutinous rice flour can be finicky. If you're having problems with the dough in your microwave, try it over a double boiler on the stove.

— Katie

STEP 1

STEP 2

STEP 3

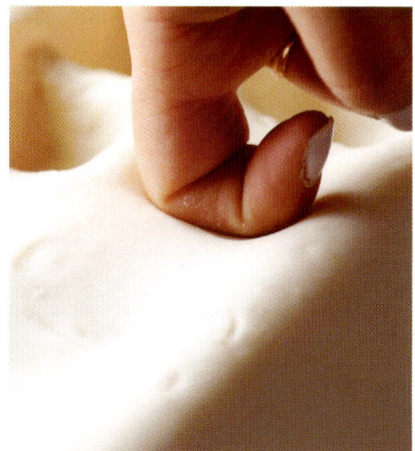

STEP 4

STEP 5

STEP 6

STEP 7

DIRECTIONS:

1. Cover a 12-cube ice tray with cooking spray. In a microwave-safe bowl, whisk the rice flour and sugar with 1½ cups water. Cover the bowl with plastic wrap and poke holes to vent. Microwave **2 minutes**.

2. The mixture will thicken into dough. Let cool, then divide in half. Roll out each with a rolling pin on a floured surface.

3. Lay a sheet of dough over the tray and gently knuckle it in.

4. Scoop ice cream into each pocket.

5. Cover the tray with the remaining dough. Freeze **1 hour**.

6. Flip the ice cube tray to release the mochi, and cut the cubes using a pizza cutter.

7. Trim the excess dough around the edges, sprinkle with garnish, and serve!

EXCLUSIVE CONTENT

SCAN HERE FOR MORE TIPS AND HACKS!

Working with Ice Cream 101

Watch the recipe video

SERVES 9-12

MOLTEN LAVA CUBES

These were made for adding **gooey** centers and next-level flavor to cookies, cakes, and more, but we've totally eaten them as is and #NoRegrets.

INGREDIENTS:

2 tbsp heavy cream

1 large candy bar of your choice (we used Hershey's Cookies 'n' Creme Bars, Reese's Peanut Butter Cups, and Snickers)

"

What's fun about these is they can be added to any kind of dessert. Mix and match with any candy bar and your favorite cookie, brownie, or cake. You can even drop one into a cup of coffee!

— Rachel

STEP 1

STEP 2

STEP 3

STEP 4

DIRECTIONS:

1. Break up the bar and place it in a microwave-safe bowl with the cream. Microwave on high for **1 minute**.

2. Remove and stir. The mixture should feel slightly thick like ganache. If it's too soupy, add more chocolate. If it's too thick, add more cream.

3. Pour the ganache into a small-cube ice tray and refrigerate until completely set, about **1 hour**.

4. When ready to use, release the cubes and add them to one of these desserts!

Use a mini-cube tray to keep your lava cubes to a single serving, if you only have a standard-size tray, just chop the finished cubes in half.

Pop it, don't stop it!

Here are some of our favorite ways to make good desserts great.

① RED VELVET LAVA CAKE

INGREDIENTS:

Cooking spray
Red-velvet cake mix, prepared
1 Cookies 'n' Creme lava cube
Powdered sugar

1. Spray your microwave-safe mug and add the cake mix. Add your lava cube.

2. Cook on high for **1 minute**. Let cool and turn the mug over to release the cake. Plate, sprinkle with powdered sugar, and serve.

② PEANUT BUTTER CHOCOLATE CHIP COOKIES

INGREDIENTS:

Store-bought refrigerated chocolate chip cookie dough, portioned
Reese's Peanut Butter Cup lava cubes

1. Completely cover each lava cube with a cookie dough portion, forming a ball. Place on a greased baking pan.

2. Bake according to the package. Let cool and serve.

③ LOADED SNICKERS BROWNIES

INGREDIENTS:

Brownie batter, prepared
Snickers lava cubes

1. Pour the brownie batter into your baking pan. Put a lava cube in place for each brownie portion. Use a spatula to smooth the batter over the top to cover.

2. Bake according to your package or recipe. Let cool. Cut, making sure the candy is in the center of each piece, and serve.

MAKE IT VEGAN

This technique will work for any brownies! Try it with your favorite vegan recipe or mix.

Use good-quality aluminum foil for the best result.

Watch the recipe video

SERVES 10-15

ALL-THE-EDGES BROWNIES

Hoarding the end pieces won't win you any friends, but with this **foil trick**, there's plenty for everyone.

INGREDIENTS:
1 package brownie mix, prepared

Rather than a cooking spray or something that may alter the flavor of what you're baking, try a magic pan release using ingredients from your recipe: In a small bowl, add butter and a piece of chocolate. Heat in the microwave for 20 or 30 seconds, mix it together, and coat your pan before you add your batter.

— *Ira*

STEP 1

STEP 2

STEP 3

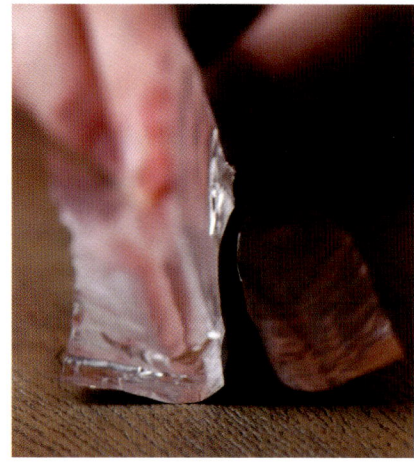

STEP 4

STEP 5

STEP 6

DIRECTIONS:

1. Preheat the oven according to the package instructions. Cut a piece of aluminum foil approximately 4 x 10 inches.

2. Fold the foil in half crosswise.

3. Fold each side in half again, creating a stand so the foil will stay upright. Repeat with two more foil sheets.

4. Attach one end of each piece to the side of a nonstick 9 x 13-inch baking pan.

5. Pour in the batter, and allow it to settle in around the foil.

6. Bake according to package instructions, let cool, and slice, removing the foil.

EXCLUSIVE CONTENT!

USE THE HACK WITH

Tahini Brownies

Trend alert: Add the ingredient of the moment to your brownies for a nutty, savory element and a gorgeous swirl too. Scan here to watch this hack.

MAKE IT VEGAN

Swap in a vegan brownie recipe, vegan ice cream, and vegan chocolate for dipping.

Watch the recipe video

SERVES 6

DOUBLE-DIP BROWNIE ICE CREAM POPS

There are so many layers of **delicious** here we've lost count. Yet these are deceptively simple to pull off.

INGREDIENTS:

2 pints cookies and cream ice cream, softened

2 packages brownie mix, prepared and baked in square pans, but not cut

7 oz dark chocolate, melted

5 oz white chocolate, melted

2 Oreos

"

Working with ice cream on a cake can be tricky because it melts quickly. To help, put the brownies in the freezer for 10 minutes before you add the ice cream, so you're working on a cold surface.

– Ira

STEP 1

STEP 2

STEP 3

STEP 4

STEP 5

STEP 6

DIRECTIONS:

1. Place 9 scoops of ice cream on the first brownie layer and spread it evenly.

2. Cover with the second brownie layer.

3. Place 6 ice pop sticks (3 on each side) into the ice cream and cut the brownie into 6 pieces. Freeze for **20 minutes**.

4. Dip each brownie pop in the dark chocolate. Refrigerate until the chocolate sets, about **10 minutes**.

5. Dip a corner of each brownie pop in the white chocolate. Refrigerate until the chocolate sets, about **10 minutes**.

6. Decorate each pop with an Oreo (use remaining melted chocolate to help it stick). Freeze for **30 minutes** before serving.

HOW TO
MAKE ICE CREAM IN A MASON JAR

Scan here to watch us get it done in just 20 minutes!

SERVES 9-12

FUDGY PRETZEL CRUST BROWNIES

Our new love language is these gooey treats. Pretzels give them a **salty crunch**.

INGREDIENTS:

1 cup butter, melted

1 tbsp coconut oil

1 cup sugar

2 eggs

2 tsp vanilla extract

1 cup flour

½ cup unsweetened cocoa powder

¼ tsp salt

¾ cup butterscotch chips

1 cup crushed pretzels

½ cup brown sugar

¼ tsp baking soda

Melted caramel, for drizzling

Melted chocolate, for drizzling

12 chocolate-covered pretzels

While there is butter in the crust that will grease the pan somewhat, to be safe, line your baking dish with parchment and let it hang over on two sides. Once the brownies are baked, you can grab both sides of the paper and lift them out, rather than damage them trying to remove them with a spatula.

— *Ira*

STEP 1

STEP 2

STEP 3

STEP 4

STEP 5

STEP 6

DIRECTIONS:

1. Preheat the oven to **350°**. In a large bowl, beat ½ cup of the butter with the coconut oil and sugar until light and fluffy, about **1 minute**.

2. Add the eggs and vanilla, and beat until pale in color, about **2 minutes** more.

3. Add ½ cup of the flour, plus the cocoa powder and salt, and combine, but don't over mix. Fold in the butterscotch chips.

4. In a medium bowl, combine the remaining ½ cup butter and ½ cup flour with the crushed pretzels, brown sugar, and baking soda. Pat the mixture in an 8 x 8-inch pan to create the crust.

5. Pour the batter over the crust and smooth it out. Bake for **25 minutes**, until set but still fudgy.

6. Let cool and remove from the pan by lifting the parchment. Drizzle with caramel and chocolate, and decorate with chocolate-covered pretzels. Cut and serve.

HOW TO MAKE
BROWNIE ICE CREAM BOWLS

Scan here to see us whip up these adorable mini sundaes, plus more brownie hacks!

Watch the recipe video

+ plus freezing time

SERVES 9

#TBT COOKIES AND CREAM CRUNCH BOMBS

Cue the nostalgia with this **no-bake dessert** featuring the treats of our youth.

INGREDIENTS:

9 Rice Krispies treat squares (from our treat sheet recipe or store-bought)

2 pints cookies and cream ice cream, softened

7 oz dark chocolate, melted

7 oz Hershey's Cookies and Creme candy (1 giant bar or about 5 regular bars), melted

You can play with this recipe, substituting different cereals and ice creams like Fruity Pebbles with strawberry ice cream or Cocoa Krispies with chocolate ice cream.

— Katie

STEP 1

STEP 2

STEP 3

STEP 4

STEP 5

DIRECTIONS:

1. Press the treats flat by rolling with a tall glass.

2. Place a small scoop of ice cream in the center of each rectangle. Wrap the scoop with the treat to form a ball. Repeat with the rest.

3. Dip one half of each ball in dark chocolate. Lay them on waxed paper and freeze for **15 minutes** to set.

4. Dip the other half in the Cookies and Creme candy.

5. Freeze again to set, about **15 minutes**, and serve.

If you don't have a rolling pin handy, use a drinking glass or even a bottle of wine.

HOW TO
MAKE A TREAT SHEET FAST

Hint: We microwaved it.

WHAT YOU NEED:

34 oz box Rice Krispies cereal
10 oz bag mini marshmallows
1 stick unsalted butter

DIRECTIONS:

1. Pour all ingredients into a large microwave-safe bowl and cook on high for 1 minute, or until the marshmallows and butter are completely melted.

2. Stir the mixture, pour it into a half-sheet pan, and refrigerate until completely cool, about 30 minutes.

Use a mason jar lid as a tool to cut perfect circles!

Watch the recipe video

SERVES 6

CRISPY CHEESECAKE BITES

Cute, handheld **creamy-crunchy** cheesecakes that can be assembled in minutes? Yes please.

INGREDIENTS:

1 Rice Krispies treat sheet (see page 75 for the recipe)

1 cup strawberry jam

1 cup cheesecake batter

¼ cup strawberry syrup

> I'm the biggest fan of cheesecake, and this is the fastest and most fun way to make it. The tools you need (a mason jar lid, a glass, a muffin tin) are things I always have in my kitchen. You can customize with different flavors—lemon, chocolate chip, caramel—the possibilities are endless.
>
> — Logan

STEP 1

STEP 2

STEP 3

STEP 4

DIRECTIONS:

1. Use a mason jar lid to cut 6 circles out of the treat sheet. Re-mold the remaining treats and use them to make other desserts (see page 72)!

2. Place the circles onto a muffin tin and use a small jar or a spoon to press them in.

3. Place about 1 tbsp jam in each indentation, followed by 1 tbsp cheesecake batter, topped with dots of strawberry syrup.

4. Drag a skewer through the dots to make a swirly decoration. Refrigerate for **1 hour**, and serve.

VEGAN

USE THE HACK WITH

Easy vegan Cheesecake

Use your blender to whip up this delicious dairy-free option in just 15 minutes (plus freezing time). Scan here to watch us make it.

Watch the recipe video

SERVES 12

STRAWBERRY ICE CREAM CRISPWICHES

I scream, you scream, we all scream for **rainbow ice cream** sandwiches.

INGREDIENTS:

2 Rice Krispies treat sheets (see page 75 for the recipe)

1 pint fresh strawberries, sliced

1 pint strawberry ice cream, softened

10 oz white chocolate, melted

Rainbow sprinkles

"

If you don't want to make a big batch, this idea is totally doable with individual treats. You can cut them from the treat sheet, or use store-bought treat squares.

— Katie

STEP 1

STEP 2

STEP 3

STEP 4

DIRECTIONS:

1. On one treat sheet, layer the sliced strawberries. Scoop the ice cream on top.

2. Spread the ice cream evenly, top with the second treat sheet, and slice into rectangles.

3. Dip each rectangle halfway into the white chocolate and immediately into the sprinkles.

4. Allow to set on waxed paper, and keep in the freezer until ready to serve.

HOW TO GET PERFECT STRAWBERRY SLICES

Like a pro.

WHAT YOU NEED:

Strawberries
Knife
Egg slicer

DIRECTIONS:

1. Wash the berries and pat them dry. Slice off the tops with a sharp knife.

2. Place each berry in the egg slicer and press.

3. Use the slices to fill your Crispwiches, decorate cakes, add to fruit salad, etc.

 Watch the recipe video

SERVES 8

SMART COOKIE HACKS

We challenged ourselves to come up with the most **fun** and **artful** ways to reinvent a roll of store-bought cookie dough in three steps or less. Cookie swap, we're coming for you.

INGREDIENTS:

1 roll store-bought refrigerated sugar cookie dough

"

Freeze your dough for 5 minutes after each step (stamping, cutting). It will maintain crisp lines all the way around the cookies and helps keep them from spreading while baking.

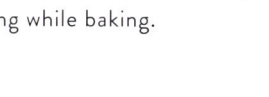

2 Step   CUT + BAKE

SWANS

TOOL: Paring knife

CUT

BAKE

2 Step STAMP + BAKE

SPIDERWEBS

TOOL: Spider frying strainer

STAMP   **BAKE**

SEASHELLS

TOOL: Sunburst lid

STAMP   **BAKE**

GLASS PRINTS

TOOL: Drinking glass with decorative bottom

STAMP   **BAKE**

3 Step STAMP + CUT + BAKE

BUTTONS

TOOLS: Drinking straw + Plastic bottle cap

STAMP **CUT** **BAKE**

HONEYCOMBS

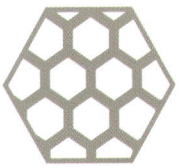

TOOLS: Bubble wrap + Paring knife

STAMP **CUT** **BAKE**

3 Step DIP + STAMP + BAKE

FLOWERS

TOOL: Small silicone whisk **INGREDIENT:** Freeze-dried raspberry powder

DIP

STAMP

BAKE

SUNBURSTS

TOOL: Fork **INGREDIENT:** Cocoa powder

DIP

STAMP

BAKE

COCOA MUSHROOMS

TOOL: Beer bottle **INGREDIENT:** Cocoa powder

DIP

STAMP

BAKE

Watch the recipe video

 VEGAN

+ plus freezing time
SERVES 12

COCO-ORANGE ICE POPS

Name a more iconic summer duo than **coconut** and **orange** —we'll wait.

INGREDIENTS:

2 16 oz cans frozen orange juice concentrate, thawed

2 13.5 oz cans coconut cream

TOOLS:

12 4 oz plastic cups

12 1 oz plastic cups

12 ice pop sticks

"

You can easily switch this up while keeping it vegan by swapping out the orange concentrate for lime concentrate, pineapple juice, or chocolate almond milk.

— Logan

STEP 1

STEP 2

STEP 3

STEP 4

STEP 5

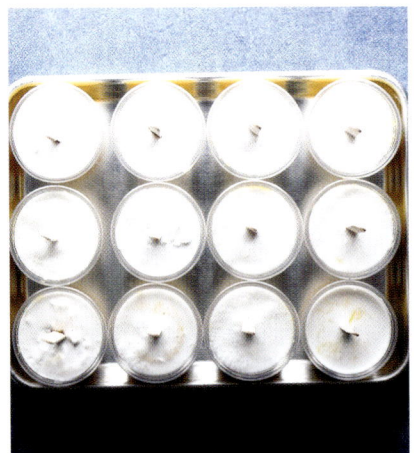

STEP 6

DIRECTIONS:

1. Pour the orange concentrate into the larger cups, filling ¾ of the way.

2. Press the small cups into the orange concentrate, then pour water into the small cups to weigh them down. Freeze until set.

3. Remove the small cups.

4. Pour in the coconut cream until it fills the rest of the large cup. The ratio of orange to coconut is up to you!

5. Add sticks to each pop, and freeze until the coconut cream sets.

6. Serve over ice—friends can remove the plastic cup when they're ready to eat.

HOW TO
MAKE ICE-POP TUBES FROM A FREEZER BAG

Pool party, right this way.

WHAT YOU NEED:

Gallon-size plastic freezer bags
Lighter
Table knife

DIRECTIONS:

1. Lay a freezer bag on your work surface.

2. Run a lighter over your knife.

3. While the knife is still hot, cut the freezer bag into even strips. The heat seals the bag shut on each side.

MAKE THESE WITH RUM!
Blueberry Mojito Ice Pops

DIY boozy frozen treats are so much fresher and yummier than the store-bought version. Scan here to watch us make them.

SERVES 20-25

FURRY COOKIE MONSTER CAKE

C is for cake! Our **frosting hack** will help you pull off this adorable textured design without special tools. Kiddos will nom-nom it up.

INGREDIENTS:

10-inch round store-bought cake with vanilla frosting

Blue frosting

6 chocolate chip cookies

2 jumbo marshmallows

2 round black candies

No need for a piping tip or piping bags.

"

If you want the fur to look short, let the frosting fall straight down naturally and swirl right onto the cake. If you want it to look longer, pull the bag to the side as you squeeze. You can also play with the design by adding more holes to the bag.

— Tennille

STEP 1

STEP 2

STEP 3

DIRECTIONS:

1. At the bottom corner of a plastic sandwich bag, puncture two holes with a fork.

2. Fill the bag with blue frosting, and pipe the cake.

3. Break the chocolate chip cookies in half and place them at the mouth, to create the illusion that it's stuffed with cookies. Add the marshmallows and black candies for eyes, using a little frosting as your glue.

FUN FACT

Is it "frosting" or is it "icing"? Like a cake itself, there are lots of ways to slice it. Frosting tends to be fluffy, which makes it ideal for creative cake decorating. Icing is usually thinner, and may be poured onto a cake or cookie for a shinier finish. Yet some say the terms are interchangeable and it depends on where you come from. "Icing" tends to be a more popular term among Southerners, while Midwesterners and West Coasters prefer "frosting." In the Northeast, it's about even. No matter what, they have one thing in common, sugar, and we're here for it.

Watch the recipe video

FRESH FLOWER CASCADE CAKE

Don't worry, you don't have to bake. Buy the layers, assemble them, then transform them into a **work of art**.

INGREDIENTS:

Store-bought cake layers with vanilla frosting (we used 6-inch, 8-inch, and 10-inch)

Vanilla frosting to match the store-bought cake

TOOLS:

Fresh flowers and greenery of your choice

Toothpicks

A toothpick is the key to securing your flower in place. It elongates the stem, allowing for a more stable connection to the cake. Also, you avoid sticking flower stems directly into your delicious creation!

— Tess

STEP 1

STEP 2

STEP 3

STEP 4

STEP 5

STEP 6

DIRECTIONS:

1. Stack your cakes (see our hack for making sure they stay upright).

2. Starting at the top, slice a piece of cake out of each layer, getting larger as you go down, creating a graduated opening.

3. Frost the cake opening to match the rest of the cake. Select a flower and trim the stem down to an inch or so.

4. Insert a toothpick into the stem.

5. Insert the toothpick into the cake.

6. Repeat with flowers and greenery until you get the look you want. Beautiful!

HOW TO KEEP YOUR MULTI-LAYER CAKE FROM FALLING

Like, whoa.

WHAT YOU NEED:

Frosted cake tiers
Smoothie straws (for a 3-layer cake you'll need 3 or 4) Scissors

DIRECTIONS:

1. Snip the straws in half.
2. Insert 3 straw pieces into the bottom layer of cake in a triangle pattern near the center. Place the next layer on top.
3. Repeat.

HOW TO MAKE Pull-Apart Cakes

Prefer edible flowers? Scan here for how to decorate beautiful floral cupcake cakes.

Watch the recipe video

STRAIGHT FIRE CAKE

Replicate these **gorgeous** flames, or customize the hack to fit any cake size and color scheme.

INGREDIENTS:

Candy melts in colors of your choice (we used red, white, and blues)

Vanilla frosting

Store-bought cake layers with vanilla frosting (we used 6-inch, 8-inch, and 10-inch)

Fresh fruit (we used blueberries, blackberries, and raspberries)

Candy melts work best for getting beautiful, vibrant colors—dyeing white chocolate yourself is tricky because it can get clumpy and grainy. If you prefer to go with chocolate, be sure to use gel food coloring—it's far less likely to seize. And go slowly when adding it so everything stays nice and smooth.

— Tess

STEP 1

STEP 2

STEP 3

STEP 4

STEP 5

STEP 6

DIRECTIONS:

1. Stack your cakes—see our hack on page 101 for making sure they stay upright.

2. Place your candy melts in microwave-safe bowls. Alternately microwave and stir until melted—watch our exclusive Candy Melts 101 video for tips!

3. Using a pastry brush, create paint strokes on your baking pan. Let them set until cool and solid, then remove. These are your flames!

4. Using dabs of frosting as your glue, attach the flames around your cake, layering them as you like.

5. Drizzle the remaining candy melts over the cake.

6. Garnish with fruit.

EXCLUSIVE CONTENT!

≡ Candy Melts 101 ≡

Before you start decorating, scan here to watch us spill the key do's and don'ts for getting the look you want.

Copyright © 2019 by First Media
All rights reserved. No part of this publication may be reproduced, distributed, or transmitted in any form or by any means, including photocopying, recording, or other electronic or mechanical methods, without the prior written permission of the publisher, except in the case of brief quotations embodied in critical reviews and certain other noncommercial uses permitted by copyright law.

Images used under license from istockphoto.com